Join Our Team
Achieve a Dream
Knowledge Changes You
You Change the World

SMART (A) GRADES
NEXT EVOLUTION BRAIN POWER REVOLUTION

What's Inside?

✔ Academic Calendar

✔ Take Great Class Notes

✔ Active Listening Skills

✔ Write Daily Test Review Notes

✔ Use Association Cues for Instant and Total Recall

✔ Convert Facts into Test Questions

✔ Review for Retention, Recognition, and Recall

✔ Self-Test for Instant and Total Recall

✔ Power Study Snacks

✔ Grade Tracker

WE ARE THE FUTURE
EVERYBODY IS SOMEBODY SPECIAL

SMARTGRADES Due Dates

Academic Calendar: August-January

August

Class	What's Due?	Due Date

Back to School: Get Organized, Prepare Study Room, Purchase School Supplies

----

September

October

November

December

January

Academic Calendar: February-June

February

Class	What's Due?	Due Date
------	------	------
------	------	------
------	------	------

March

------	------	------
------	------	------
------	------	------

April

------	------	------
------	------	------
------	------	------

May

------	------	------
------	------	------
------	------	------

June

------	------	------
------	------	------

Superhighway of Academic Success

The Academic Facts Move from a Blackboard, to a Notebook, to a Homework Assignment, Through Your Powerful Brain, and to a Test

Learn to Listen and Listen to Learn

SMARTGRADES In-Class Active Listening Skills

1. Pre-read the lecture topic. ✔

2. Clear your mind of all distractions (thoughts, feelings: worry, anxiety, and fear). ✔

3. Focus. Follow the speaker's line of argument. ✔

4. Selectively listen for the key facts, phrases, and words. ✔

5. What does the speaker focus on? Concepts? Formulas? ✔

6. As questions arise, write them down in the margins of your notebook. ✔

7. Ask your teacher for clarification. ✔

8. Do not leave class feeling lost, confused, or hopeless. ✔

Plan Your Work and Work Your Plan

SMARTGRADES In-Class Note Taking Skills

1. Take organized notes: Write down the main ideas and supporting details. ✔

2. To write quickly, use abbreviations and shorthand symbols. ✔

3. Bring extra pens and pencils. ✔

4. Write the homework assignment down in a SMARTGRADES Academic Assignment Planner (not in your head) and double check it for accuracy. ✔

Failing to Prepare Is Preparing to Fail

SMARTGRADES After-Class Test Review Notes to Ace Your Test

1. Choose a study area that is free of external and social distractions: _____ ✔

2. Eat a **Power Study Snack** to stay energized and focused (see list): _____ ✔

3. **Manage your time.** ✔
Estimate Time (Fantasy):   Start Time: Finish Time: **Actual Time (Reality):**

4. After every class, read your class notes and underline/highlight the <u>main ideas</u> and <u>supporting details.</u> ✔

5. **Condensation** (Distillation): Outline/summarize your class notes into **Test Review Notes.** ✔

6. Do the facts need further clarification (see another textbook, tutoring center, or teacher)? ✔

7. Visualize the test question. Convert the facts into a test question: Define Terms? Compare? Contrast? Cause and Effect? Pros and Cons? List? Prove? Discuss? Outline? Agree or Disagree? ✔

8. Use **Association Cues** to memorize facts for **Instant and Total Recall.** Attach an unknown fact to a known fact stored in your memory. Use very personal memories for higher rates of retention. ✔

Acrostic Cue: Use a sentence to condense the key facts. For example, to remember the order of G-clef notes on sheet music, (E, G, B, D, F,) use the classic acrostic: Every Good Boy Deserves Fun.

Rhyme Cue: Use rhymes to link the key facts together. For example, the classic, "I before E, except after C."

Music Cue: Make up a song or poem with the information in it. Sing the song or recite the poem several times.

Chaining Cue: Create a story where each word or idea you have to remember cues the next idea you need to recall. Use your imagination. If you had to remember the name, Shirley Temple, you could rhyme Shirley with curly and remember that she had curly hair around her temples.

Funny Cue: Write a joke that contains the key facts. The funniest, most outlandish, and the strangest concoction of memory cues makes memorizing easy.

9. Two weeks before the test, **Self-Test** for strengths and weaknesses (change weak cues). ✔

10. The day of the test, review your study notes to refresh your memory. Ace the Test. ✔

Take Control of Your Day, Your Dream and Your Destiny!

Date:

Topic:

Write down the Main Ideas and Supporting Details/Examples/Arguments:

_____

_____

_____

_____

_____

_____

_____

_____

_____

_____

_____

_____

_____

_____

_____

_____

_____

_____

_____

_____

_____

_____

_____

_____

_____

_____

_____

_____

_____

_____

_____

_____

After Class, Write Test Review Note: Association Cues and Test Questions

1. After class, reread your class notes and condense them into Test Review Notes ✓

2. Choose a study area that is free of external and social distractions: _____ ✓

3. Eat a Power Study Snack to stay energized and focused (see list): _____ ✓

4. Manage your time.
   Estimate Time (Fantasy):   Start Time: Finish Time: Actual Time (Reality): ✓

5. Do the facts need further clarification (see textbook, tutoring center, or teacher)? ✓

6. To ace your test, use Association Cues to memorize the facts for Instant and Total Recall ✓

Fact: Create Association Cue for Instant and Total Recall

----

7. Visualize the test questions. Convert the facts into test questions ✓

Who? Where? When? What? Why?

Date:

Topic:

Write down the Main Ideas and Supporting Details/Examples/Arguments:

_____

_____

_____

_____

_____

_____

_____

_____

_____

_____

_____

_____

_____

_____

_____

_____

_____

_____

_____

_____

_____

_____

_____

_____

_____

_____

_____

_____

_____

_____

_____

_____

_____

_____

_____

After Class, Write Test Review Note: Association Cues and Test Questions

1. After class, reread your class notes and condense them into Test Review Notes ✔

2. Choose a study area that is free of external and social distractions: _____ ✔

3. Eat a Power Study Snack to stay energized and focused (see list): _____ ✔

4. Manage your time.
   Estimate Time (Fantasy):   Start Time: Finish Time: Actual Time (Reality): ✔

5. Do the facts need further clarification (see textbook, tutoring center, or teacher)? ✔

6. To ace your test, use Association Cues to memorize the facts for Instant and Total Recall ✔

Fact: Create Association Cue for Instant and Total Recall

----

7. Visualize the test questions. Convert the facts into test questions ✔

Who? Where? When? What? Why?

My Class Notes

Date:

Topic:

Write down the Main Ideas and Supporting Details/Examples/Arguments:

After Class, Write Test Review Note: Association Cues and Test Questions

1. After class, reread your class notes and condense them into Test Review Notes ✔

2. Choose a study area that is free of external and social distractions: _____ ✔

3. Eat a Power Study Snack to stay energized and focused (see list): _____ ✔

4. Manage your time.
   Estimate Time (Fantasy):   Start Time: Finish Time: Actual Time (Reality): ✔

5. Do the facts need further clarification (see textbook, tutoring center, or teacher)? ✔

6. To ace your test, use Association Cues to memorize the facts for Instant and Total Recall ✔

Fact: Create Association Cue for Instant and Total Recall

----

7. Visualize the test questions. Convert the facts into test questions ✔

Who? Where? When? What? Why?

My Class Notes

Date:

Topic:

Write down the Main Ideas and Supporting Details/Examples/Arguments:

_____

_____

_____

_____

_____

_____

_____

_____

_____

_____

_____

_____

_____

_____

_____

_____

_____

_____

_____

_____

_____

_____

_____

_____

_____

_____

_____

_____

_____

_____

_____

_____

_____

_____

_____

After Class, Write Test Review Note: Association Cues and Test Questions

1. After class, reread your class notes and condense them into Test Review Notes ✔

2. Choose a study area that is free of external and social distractions: _____ ✔

3. Eat a Power Study Snack to stay energized and focused (see list): _____ ✔

4. Manage your time.
   Estimate Time (Fantasy):   Start Time: Finish Time: Actual Time (Reality): ✔

5. Do the facts need further clarification (see textbook, tutoring center, or teacher)? ✔

6. To ace your test, use Association Cues to memorize the facts for Instant and Total Recall ✔

Fact: Create Association Cue for Instant and Total Recall

----

7. Visualize the test questions. Convert the facts into test questions ✔

Who? Where? When? What? Why?

My Class Notes

Date:

Topic:

Write down the Main Ideas and Supporting Details/Examples/Arguments:

_____

_____

_____

_____

_____

_____

_____

_____

_____

_____

_____

_____

_____

_____

_____

_____

_____

_____

_____

_____

_____

_____

_____

_____

_____

_____

_____

_____

_____

_____

_____

_____

_____

After Class, Write Test Review Note: Association Cues and Test Questions

1. After class, reread your class notes and condense them into Test Review Notes ✓

2. Choose a study area that is free of external and social distractions: _____ ✓

3. Eat a Power Study Snack to stay energized and focused (see list): _____ ✓

4. Manage your time.
   Estimate Time (Fantasy):   Start Time: Finish Time: Actual Time (Reality): ✓

5. Do the facts need further clarification (see textbook, tutoring center, or teacher)? ✓

6. To ace your test, use Association Cues to memorize the facts for Instant and Total Recall ✓

Fact: Create Association Cue for Instant and Total Recall

----

7. Visualize the test questions. Convert the facts into test questions ✓

Who? Where? When? What? Why?

My Class Notes

Date:

Topic:

Write down the Main Ideas and Supporting Details/Examples/Arguments:

_____

_____

_____

_____

_____

_____

_____

_____

_____

_____

_____

_____

_____

_____

_____

_____

_____

_____

_____

_____

_____

_____

_____

_____

_____

_____

_____

_____

_____

_____

_____

_____

_____

_____

_____

_____

_____

_____

My Class Notes

Write down the Main Ideas and Supporting Details/Examples/Arguments:

_____

After Class, Write Test Review Note: Association Cues and Test Questions

1. After class, reread your class notes and condense them into Test Review Notes ✔

2. Choose a study area that is free of external and social distractions: _____ ✔

3. Eat a Power Study Snack to stay energized and focused (see list): _____ ✔

4. Manage your time.
   Estimate Time (Fantasy):   Start Time: Finish Time: Actual Time (Reality): ✔

5. Do the facts need further clarification (see textbook, tutoring center, or teacher)? ✔

6. To ace your test, use Association Cues to memorize the facts for Instant and Total Recall ✔

Fact: Create Association Cue for Instant and Total Recall

- -

7. Visualize the test questions. Convert the facts into test questions ✔

Who? Where? When? What? Why?

My Class Notes

Date:

Topic:

Write down the Main Ideas and Supporting Details/Examples/Arguments:

_____

_____

_____

_____

_____

_____

_____

_____

_____

_____

_____

_____

_____

_____

_____

_____

_____

_____

_____

_____

_____

_____

_____

_____

_____

_____

_____

_____

_____

_____

_____

_____

_____

_____

Write down the Main Ideas and Supporting Details/Examples/Arguments:

After Class, Write Test Review Note: Association Cues and Test Questions

1. After class, reread your class notes and condense them into Test Review Notes ✓

2. Choose a study area that is free of external and social distractions: _____ ✓

3. Eat a Power Study Snack to stay energized and focused (see list): _____ ✓

4. Manage your time.
   Estimate Time (Fantasy):   Start Time: Finish Time: Actual Time (Reality): ✓

5. Do the facts need further clarification (see textbook, tutoring center, or teacher)? ✓

6. To ace your test, use Association Cues to memorize the facts for Instant and Total Recall ✓

Fact: Create Association Cue for Instant and Total Recall

----

7. Visualize the test questions. Convert the facts into test questions ✓

Who? Where? When? What? Why?

My Class Notes

Date:

Topic:

Write down the Main Ideas and Supporting Details/Examples/Arguments:

_____

_____

_____

_____

_____

_____

_____

_____

_____

_____

_____

_____

_____

_____

_____

_____

_____

_____

_____

_____

_____

_____

_____

_____

_____

_____

_____

_____

_____

_____

_____

_____

_____

_____

_____

_____

_____

_____

After Class, Write Test Review Note: Association Cues and Test Questions

1. After class, reread your class notes and condense them into Test Review Notes ✔

2. Choose a study area that is free of external and social distractions: _____ ✔

3. Eat a Power Study Snack to stay energized and focused (see list): _____ ✔

4. Manage your time.
   Estimate Time (Fantasy):   Start Time: Finish Time: Actual Time (Reality): ✔

5. Do the facts need further clarification (see textbook, tutoring center, or teacher)? ✔

6. To ace your test, use Association Cues to memorize the facts for Instant and Total Recall ✔

Fact: Create Association Cue for Instant and Total Recall

---

7. Visualize the test questions. Convert the facts into test questions ✔

Who? Where? When? What? Why?

Date:

Topic:

Write down the Main Ideas and Supporting Details/Examples/Arguments:

_____

_____

_____

_____

_____

_____

_____

_____

_____

_____

_____

_____

_____

_____

_____

_____

_____

_____

_____

_____

_____

_____

_____

_____

_____

_____

_____

_____

_____

_____

_____

_____

_____

_____

After Class, Write Test Review Note: Association Cues and Test Questions

1. After class, reread your class notes and condense them into Test Review Notes ✔

2. Choose a study area that is free of external and social distractions: _____ ✔

3. Eat a Power Study Snack to stay energized and focused (see list): _____ ✔

4. Manage your time.
   Estimate Time (Fantasy):   Start Time: Finish Time: Actual Time (Reality): ✔

5. Do the facts need further clarification (see textbook, tutoring center, or teacher)? ✔

6. To ace your test, use Association Cues to memorize the facts for Instant and Total Recall ✔

Fact: Create Association Cue for Instant and Total Recall

- -

7. Visualize the test questions. Convert the facts into test questions ✔

Who? Where? When? What? Why?

My Class Notes

Date:

Topic:

Write down the Main Ideas and Supporting Details/Examples/Arguments:

_____

_____

_____

_____

_____

_____

_____

_____

_____

_____

_____

_____

_____

_____

_____

_____

_____

_____

_____

_____

_____

_____

_____

_____

_____

_____

_____

_____

_____

_____

_____

_____

_____

_____

After Class, Write Test Review Note: Association Cues and Test Questions

1. After class, reread your class notes and condense them into Test Review Notes ✓

2. Choose a study area that is free of external and social distractions: _____ ✓

3. Eat a Power Study Snack to stay energized and focused (see list): _____ ✓

4. Manage your time.
   Estimate Time (Fantasy):   Start Time: Finish Time: Actual Time (Reality): ✓

5. Do the facts need further clarification (see textbook, tutoring center, or teacher)? ✓

6. To ace your test, use Association Cues to memorize the facts for Instant and Total Recall ✓

Fact: Create Association Cue for Instant and Total Recall

---

7. Visualize the test questions. Convert the facts into test questions ✓

Who? Where? When? What? Why?

Date:

Topic:

Write down the Main Ideas and Supporting Details/Examples/Arguments:

_____

_____

_____

_____

_____

_____

_____

_____

_____

_____

_____

_____

_____

_____

_____

_____

_____

_____

_____

_____

_____

_____

_____

_____

_____

_____

_____

_____

_____

_____

_____

After Class, Write Test Review Note: Association Cues and Test Questions

1. After class, reread your class notes and condense them into Test Review Notes ✔

2. Choose a study area that is free of external and social distractions: _____ ✔

3. Eat a Power Study Snack to stay energized and focused (see list): _____ ✔

4. Manage your time.
   Estimate Time (Fantasy):   Start Time: Finish Time: Actual Time (Reality): ✔

5. Do the facts need further clarification (see textbook, tutoring center, or teacher)? ✔

6. To ace your test, use Association Cues to memorize the facts for Instant and Total Recall ✔

Fact: Create Association Cue for Instant and Total Recall

----

7. Visualize the test questions. Convert the facts into test questions ✔

Who? Where? When? What? Why?

My Class Notes

Date:

Topic:

Write down the Main Ideas and Supporting Details/Examples/Arguments:

_____

_____

_____

_____

_____

_____

_____

_____

_____

_____

_____

_____

_____

_____

_____

_____

_____

_____

_____

_____

_____

_____

_____

_____

_____

_____

_____

_____

_____

_____

After Class, Write Test Review Note: Association Cues and Test Questions

1. After class, reread your class notes and condense them into Test Review Notes ✔

2. Choose a study area that is free of external and social distractions: _____ ✔

3. Eat a Power Study Snack to stay energized and focused (see list): _____ ✔

4. Manage your time.
   Estimate Time (Fantasy):   Start Time: Finish Time: Actual Time (Reality): ✔

5. Do the facts need further clarification (see textbook, tutoring center, or teacher)? ✔

6. To ace your test, use Association Cues to memorize the facts for Instant and Total Recall ✔

Fact: Create Association Cue for Instant and Total Recall

----

7. Visualize the test questions. Convert the facts into test questions ✔

Who? Where? When? What? Why?

Date:

Topic:

Write down the Main Ideas and Supporting Details/Examples/Arguments:

_____

_____

_____

_____

_____

_____

_____

_____

_____

_____

_____

_____

_____

_____

_____

_____

_____

_____

_____

_____

_____

_____

_____

_____

_____

_____

_____

_____

_____

_____

_____

_____

_____

After Class, Write Test Review Note: Association Cues and Test Questions

1. After class, reread your class notes and condense them into Test Review Notes ✔

2. Choose a study area that is free of external and social distractions: _____ ✔

3. Eat a Power Study Snack to stay energized and focused (see list): _____ ✔

4. Manage your time.
   Estimate Time (Fantasy):   Start Time: Finish Time: Actual Time (Reality): ✔

5. Do the facts need further clarification (see textbook, tutoring center, or teacher)? ✔

6. To ace your test, use Association Cues to memorize the facts for Instant and Total Recall ✔

Fact: Create Association Cue for Instant and Total Recall

- -

7. Visualize the test questions. Convert the facts into test questions ✔

Who? Where? When? What? Why?

Date:

Topic:

Write down the Main Ideas and Supporting Details/Examples/Arguments:

_____

_____

_____

_____

_____

_____

_____

_____

_____

_____

_____

_____

_____

_____

_____

_____

_____

_____

_____

_____

_____

_____

_____

_____

_____

_____

_____

_____

_____

_____

_____

_____

_____

_____

_____

Write down the Main Ideas and Supporting Details/Examples/Arguments:

_____

_____

After Class, Write Test Review Note: Association Cues and Test Questions

1. After class, reread your class notes and condense them into Test Review Notes ✔

2. Choose a study area that is free of external and social distractions: _____ ✔

3. Eat a Power Study Snack to stay energized and focused (see list): _____ ✔

4. Manage your time.
   Estimate Time (Fantasy):   Start Time: Finish Time: Actual Time (Reality): ✔

5. Do the facts need further clarification (see textbook, tutoring center, or teacher)? ✔

6. To ace your test, use Association Cues to memorize the facts for Instant and Total Recall ✔

Fact: Create Association Cue for Instant and Total Recall

----

7. Visualize the test questions. Convert the facts into test questions ✔

Who? Where? When? What? Why?

My Class Notes   **SMARTGRADES**

Date:

Topic:

Write down the Main Ideas and Supporting Details/Examples/Arguments:

_____

_____

_____

_____

_____

_____

_____

_____

_____

_____

_____

_____

_____

_____

_____

_____

_____

_____

_____

_____

_____

_____

_____

_____

_____

_____

_____

_____

_____

_____

My Class Notes

Date:

_____

Write down the Main Ideas and Supporting Details/Examples/Arguments:

_____

After Class, Write Test Review Note: Association Cues and Test Questions

1. After class, reread your class notes and condense them into Test Review Notes✔

2. Choose a study area that is free of external and social distractions: _____ ✔

3. Eat a Power Study Snack to stay energized and focused (see list): _____ ✔

4. Manage your time.
   Estimate Time (Fantasy):   Start Time: Finish Time: Actual Time (Reality):✔

5. Do the facts need further clarification (see textbook, tutoring center, or teacher)? ✔

6. To ace your test, use Association Cues to memorize the facts for Instant and Total Recall✔

Fact: Create Association Cue for Instant and Total Recall

- -

7. Visualize the test questions. Convert the facts into test questions ✔

Who? Where? When? What? Why?

My Class Notes

Date:

Topic:

Write down the Main Ideas and Supporting Details/Examples/Arguments:

_____
_____
_____
_____
_____
_____
_____
_____
_____
_____
_____
_____
_____
_____
_____
_____
_____
_____
_____
_____
_____
_____
_____
_____
_____
_____
_____
_____
_____
_____

After Class, Write Test Review Note: Association Cues and Test Questions

1. After class, reread your class notes and condense them into Test Review Notes ✓

2. Choose a study area that is free of external and social distractions: _____ ✓

3. Eat a Power Study Snack to stay energized and focused (see list): _____ ✓

4. Manage your time.
   Estimate Time (Fantasy):   Start Time: Finish Time: Actual Time (Reality): ✓

5. Do the facts need further clarification (see textbook, tutoring center, or teacher)? ✓

6. To ace your test, use Association Cues to memorize the facts for Instant and Total Recall ✓

Fact: Create Association Cue for Instant and Total Recall

---

7. Visualize the test questions. Convert the facts into test questions ✓

Who? Where? When? What? Why?

My Class Notes

Date:

Topic:

Write down the Main Ideas and Supporting Details/Examples/Arguments:

_____

_____

_____

_____

_____

_____

_____

_____

_____

_____

_____

_____

_____

_____

_____

_____

_____

_____

_____

_____

_____

_____

_____

_____

_____

_____

_____

_____

_____

_____

_____

_____

_____

_____

My Class Notes

Write down the Main Ideas and Supporting Details/Examples/Arguments:

_____

After Class, Write Test Review Note: Association Cues and Test Questions

1. After class, reread your class notes and condense them into Test Review Notes ✔

2. Choose a study area that is free of external and social distractions: _____ ✔

3. Eat a Power Study Snack to stay energized and focused (see list): _____ ✔

4. Manage your time.
   Estimate Time (Fantasy):   Start Time: Finish Time: Actual Time (Reality): ✔

5. Do the facts need further clarification (see textbook, tutoring center, or teacher)? ✔

6. To ace your test, use Association Cues to memorize the facts for Instant and Total Recall ✔

Fact: Create Association Cue for Instant and Total Recall

----

7. Visualize the test questions. Convert the facts into test questions ✔

Who? Where? When? What? Why?

My Class Notes

Date:

Topic:

Write down the Main Ideas and Supporting Details/Examples/Arguments:

_____

_____

_____

_____

_____

_____

_____

_____

_____

_____

_____

_____

_____

_____

_____

_____

_____

_____

_____

_____

_____

_____

_____

_____

_____

_____

_____

_____

_____

_____

_____

_____

_____

After Class, Write Test Review Note: Association Cues and Test Questions

1. After class, reread your class notes and condense them into Test Review Notes✔

2. Choose a study area that is free of external and social distractions: _____ ✔

3. Eat a Power Study Snack to stay energized and focused (see list): _____ ✔

4. Manage your time.
   Estimate Time (Fantasy):   Start Time: Finish Time: Actual Time (Reality):✔

5. Do the facts need further clarification (see textbook, tutoring center, or teacher)? ✔

6. To ace your test, use Association Cues to memorize the facts for Instant and Total Recall✔

Fact: Create Association Cue for Instant and Total Recall

----

7. Visualize the test questions. Convert the facts into test questions ✔

Who? Where? When? What? Why?

Date:

Topic:

Write down the Main Ideas and Supporting Details/Examples/Arguments:

_____

_____

_____

_____

_____

_____

_____

_____

_____

_____

_____

_____

_____

_____

_____

_____

_____

_____

_____

_____

_____

_____

_____

_____

_____

_____

_____

_____

_____

_____

_____

After Class, Write Test Review Note: Association Cues and Test Questions

1. After class, reread your class notes and condense them into Test Review Notes ✔

2. Choose a study area that is free of external and social distractions: _____ ✔

3. Eat a Power Study Snack to stay energized and focused (see list): _____ ✔

4. Manage your time.
   Estimate Time (Fantasy):   Start Time: Finish Time: Actual Time (Reality): ✔

5. Do the facts need further clarification (see textbook, tutoring center, or teacher)? ✔

6. To ace your test, use Association Cues to memorize the facts for Instant and Total Recall ✔

Fact: Create Association Cue for Instant and Total Recall

----

7. Visualize the test questions. Convert the facts into test questions ✔

Who? Where? When? What? Why?

My Class Notes   **SMARTGRADES**

Date:

Topic:

Write down the Main Ideas and Supporting Details/Examples/Arguments:

_____
_____
_____
_____
_____
_____
_____
_____
_____
_____
_____
_____
_____
_____
_____
_____
_____
_____
_____
_____
_____
_____
_____
_____
_____
_____
_____
_____
_____
_____

After Class, Write Test Review Note: Association Cues and Test Questions

1. After class, reread your class notes and condense them into Test Review Notes ✔

2. Choose a study area that is free of external and social distractions: _____ ✔

3. Eat a Power Study Snack to stay energized and focused (see list): _____ ✔

4. Manage your time.
   Estimate Time (Fantasy):   Start Time: Finish Time: Actual Time (Reality): ✔

5. Do the facts need further clarification (see textbook, tutoring center, or teacher)? ✔

6. To ace your test, use Association Cues to memorize the facts for Instant and Total Recall ✔

Fact: Create Association Cue for Instant and Total Recall

- -

7. Visualize the test questions. Convert the facts into test questions ✔

Who? Where? When? What? Why?

My Class Notes

Date:

Topic:

Write down the Main Ideas and Supporting Details/Examples/Arguments:

_____

_____

_____

_____

_____

_____

_____

_____

_____

_____

_____

_____

_____

_____

_____

_____

_____

_____

_____

_____

_____

_____

_____

_____

_____

_____

_____

_____

_____

_____

_____

_____

_____

_____

After Class, Write Test Review Note: Association Cues and Test Questions

1. After class, reread your class notes and condense them into Test Review Notes ✓

2. Choose a study area that is free of external and social distractions: _____ ✓

3. Eat a Power Study Snack to stay energized and focused (see list): _____ ✓

4. Manage your time.
   Estimate Time (Fantasy):   Start Time: Finish Time: Actual Time (Reality): ✓

5. Do the facts need further clarification (see textbook, tutoring center, or teacher)? ✓

6. To ace your test, use Association Cues to memorize the facts for Instant and Total Recall ✓

Fact: Create Association Cue for Instant and Total Recall

- -

7. Visualize the test questions. Convert the facts into test questions ✓

Who? Where? When? What? Why?

Date:

Topic:

Write down the Main Ideas and Supporting Details/Examples/Arguments:

_____

_____

_____

_____

_____

_____

_____

_____

_____

_____

_____

_____

_____

_____

_____

_____

_____

_____

_____

_____

_____

_____

_____

_____

_____

_____

_____

_____

_____

_____

_____

_____

_____

_____

_____

After Class, Write Test Review Note: Association Cues and Test Questions

1. After class, reread your class notes and condense them into Test Review Notes ✔

2. Choose a study area that is free of external and social distractions: _____ ✔

3. Eat a Power Study Snack to stay energized and focused (see list): _____ ✔

4. Manage your time.
   Estimate Time (Fantasy):   Start Time: Finish Time: Actual Time (Reality): ✔

5. Do the facts need further clarification (see textbook, tutoring center, or teacher)? ✔

6. To ace your test, use Association Cues to memorize the facts for Instant and Total Recall ✔

Fact: Create Association Cue for Instant and Total Recall

----

7. Visualize the test questions. Convert the facts into test questions ✔

Who? Where? When? What? Why?

My Class Notes

Date:

Topic:

Write down the Main Ideas and Supporting Details/Examples/Arguments:

_____

_____

_____

_____

_____

_____

_____

_____

_____

_____

_____

_____

_____

_____

_____

_____

_____

_____

_____

_____

_____

_____

_____

_____

_____

_____

_____

_____

_____

_____

_____

_____

_____

_____

_____

After Class, Write Test Review Note: Association Cues and Test Questions

1. After class, reread your class notes and condense them into Test Review Notes ✔

2. Choose a study area that is free of external and social distractions: _____ ✔

3. Eat a Power Study Snack to stay energized and focused (see list): _____ ✔

4. Manage your time.
   Estimate Time (Fantasy):   Start Time: Finish Time: Actual Time (Reality): ✔

5. Do the facts need further clarification (see textbook, tutoring center, or teacher)? ✔

6. To ace your test, use Association Cues to memorize the facts for Instant and Total Recall ✔

Fact: Create Association Cue for Instant and Total Recall

----

7. Visualize the test questions. Convert the facts into test questions ✔

Who? Where? When? What? Why?

My Class Notes

SMARTGRADES

Date:

Topic:

Write down the Main Ideas and Supporting Details/Examples/Arguments:

_____

_____

_____

_____

_____

_____

_____

_____

_____

_____

_____

_____

_____

_____

_____

_____

_____

_____

_____

_____

_____

_____

_____

_____

_____

_____

_____

_____

_____

_____

After Class, Write Test Review Note: Association Cues and Test Questions

1. After class, reread your class notes and condense them into Test Review Notes ✔

2. Choose a study area that is free of external and social distractions: _____ ✔

3. Eat a Power Study Snack to stay energized and focused (see list): _____ ✔

4. Manage your time.
   Estimate Time (Fantasy):   Start Time: Finish Time: Actual Time (Reality): ✔

5. Do the facts need further clarification (see textbook, tutoring center, or teacher)? ✔

6. To ace your test, use Association Cues to memorize the facts for Instant and Total Recall ✔

Fact: Create Association Cue for Instant and Total Recall

- -

7. Visualize the test questions. Convert the facts into test questions ✔

Who? Where? When? What? Why?

My Class Notes

Date:

Topic:

Write down the Main Ideas and Supporting Details/Examples/Arguments:

_____

_____

_____

_____

_____

_____

_____

_____

_____

_____

_____

_____

_____

_____

_____

_____

_____

_____

_____

_____

_____

_____

_____

_____

_____

_____

_____

_____

_____

_____

_____

_____

After Class, Write Test Review Note: Association Cues and Test Questions

1. After class, reread your class notes and condense them into Test Review Notes ✓

2. Choose a study area that is free of external and social distractions: _____ ✓

3. Eat a Power Study Snack to stay energized and focused (see list): _____ ✓

4. Manage your time.
   Estimate Time (Fantasy):   Start Time: Finish Time: Actual Time (Reality): ✓

5. Do the facts need further clarification (see textbook, tutoring center, or teacher)? ✓

6. To ace your test, use Association Cues to memorize the facts for Instant and Total Recall ✓

Fact: Create Association Cue for Instant and Total Recall

----

7. Visualize the test questions. Convert the facts into test questions ✓

Who? Where? When? What? Why?

My Class Notes

Date:

Topic:

Write down the Main Ideas and Supporting Details/Examples/Arguments:

_____

_____

_____

_____

_____

_____

_____

_____

_____

_____

_____

_____

_____

_____

_____

_____

_____

_____

_____

_____

_____

_____

_____

_____

_____

_____

_____

_____

_____

_____

_____

After Class, Write Test Review Note: Association Cues and Test Questions

1. After class, reread your class notes and condense them into Test Review Notes ✔

2. Choose a study area that is free of external and social distractions: _____ ✔

3. Eat a Power Study Snack to stay energized and focused (see list): _____ ✔

4. Manage your time.
   Estimate Time (Fantasy):   Start Time: Finish Time: Actual Time (Reality): ✔

5. Do the facts need further clarification (see textbook, tutoring center, or teacher)? ✔

6. To ace your test, use Association Cues to memorize the facts for Instant and Total Recall ✔

Fact: Create Association Cue for Instant and Total Recall

----

7. Visualize the test questions. Convert the facts into test questions ✔

Who? Where? When? What? Why?

My Class Notes

Date:

Topic:

Write down the Main Ideas and Supporting Details/Examples/Arguments:

_____
_____
_____
_____
_____
_____
_____
_____
_____
_____
_____
_____
_____
_____
_____
_____
_____
_____
_____
_____
_____
_____
_____
_____
_____
_____
_____
_____
_____
_____
_____
_____
_____
_____

After Class, Write Test Review Note: Association Cues and Test Questions

1. After class, reread your class notes and condense them into Test Review Notes ✔

2. Choose a study area that is free of external and social distractions: _____ ✔

3. Eat a Power Study Snack to stay energized and focused (see list): _____ ✔

4. Manage your time.
   Estimate Time (Fantasy):   Start Time: Finish Time: Actual Time (Reality): ✔

5. Do the facts need further clarification (see textbook, tutoring center, or teacher)? ✔

6. To ace your test, use Association Cues to memorize the facts for Instant and Total Recall ✔

Fact: Create Association Cue for Instant and Total Recall

----

7. Visualize the test questions. Convert the facts into test questions ✔

Who? Where? When? What? Why?

My Class Notes

Date:

Topic:

Write down the Main Ideas and Supporting Details/Examples/Arguments:

_____
_____
_____
_____
_____
_____
_____
_____
_____
_____
_____
_____
_____
_____
_____
_____
_____
_____
_____
_____
_____
_____
_____
_____
_____
_____
_____
_____
_____
_____
_____
_____
_____

Write down the Main Ideas and Supporting Details/Examples/Arguments:

After Class, Write Test Review Note: Association Cues and Test Questions

1. After class, reread your class notes and condense them into Test Review Notes ✔

2. Choose a study area that is free of external and social distractions: _____ ✔

3. Eat a Power Study Snack to stay energized and focused (see list): _____ ✔

4. Manage your time.
   Estimate Time (Fantasy):   Start Time: Finish Time: Actual Time (Reality): ✔

5. Do the facts need further clarification (see textbook, tutoring center, or teacher)? ✔

6. To ace your test, use Association Cues to memorize the facts for Instant and Total Recall ✔

Fact: Create Association Cue for Instant and Total Recall

----

7. Visualize the test questions. Convert the facts into test questions ✔

Who? Where? When? What? Why?

My Class Notes

Date:

Topic:

Write down the Main Ideas and Supporting Details/Examples/Arguments:

_____

_____

_____

_____

_____

_____

_____

_____

_____

_____

_____

_____

_____

_____

_____

_____

_____

_____

_____

_____

_____

_____

_____

_____

_____

_____

_____

_____

_____

_____

_____

After Class, Write Test Review Note: Association Cues and Test Questions

1. After class, reread your class notes and condense them into Test Review Notes ✓

2. Choose a study area that is free of external and social distractions: _____ ✓

3. Eat a Power Study Snack to stay energized and focused (see list): _____ ✓

4. Manage your time.
   Estimate Time (Fantasy):   Start Time: Finish Time: Actual Time (Reality): ✓

5. Do the facts need further clarification (see textbook, tutoring center, or teacher)? ✓

6. To ace your test, use Association Cues to memorize the facts for Instant and Total Recall ✓

Fact: Create Association Cue for Instant and Total Recall

- -

7. Visualize the test questions. Convert the facts into test questions ✓

Who? Where? When? What? Why?

Date:

Topic:

Write down the Main Ideas and Supporting Details/Examples/Arguments:

_____

_____

_____

_____

_____

_____

_____

_____

_____

_____

_____

_____

_____

_____

_____

_____

_____

_____

_____

_____

_____

_____

_____

_____

_____

_____

_____

_____

_____

_____

_____

_____

After Class, Write Test Review Note: Association Cues and Test Questions

1. After class, reread your class notes and condense them into Test Review Notes ✔

2. Choose a study area that is free of external and social distractions: _____ ✔

3. Eat a Power Study Snack to stay energized and focused (see list): _____ ✔

4. Manage your time.
   Estimate Time (Fantasy):   Start Time: Finish Time: Actual Time (Reality): ✔

5. Do the facts need further clarification (see textbook, tutoring center, or teacher)? ✔

6. To ace your test, use Association Cues to memorize the facts for Instant and Total Recall ✔

Fact: Create Association Cue for Instant and Total Recall

----

7. Visualize the test questions. Convert the facts into test questions ✔

Who? Where? When? What? Why?

My Class Notes

Date:

Topic:

Write down the Main Ideas and Supporting Details/Examples/Arguments:

_____

_____

_____

_____

_____

_____

_____

_____

_____

_____

_____

_____

_____

_____

_____

_____

_____

_____

_____

_____

_____

_____

_____

_____

_____

_____

_____

_____

_____

_____

_____

_____

_____

_____

After Class, Write Test Review Note: Association Cues and Test Questions

1. After class, reread your class notes and condense them into Test Review Notes ✔

2. Choose a study area that is free of external and social distractions: _____ ✔

3. Eat a Power Study Snack to stay energized and focused (see list): _____ ✔

4. Manage your time.
   Estimate Time (Fantasy):   Start Time: Finish Time: Actual Time (Reality): ✔

5. Do the facts need further clarification (see textbook, tutoring center, or teacher)? ✔

6. To ace your test, use Association Cues to memorize the facts for Instant and Total Recall ✔

Fact: Create Association Cue for Instant and Total Recall

- -

7. Visualize the test questions. Convert the facts into test questions ✔

Who? Where? When? What? Why?

My Class Notes

Date:

Topic:

Write down the Main Ideas and Supporting Details/Examples/Arguments:

_____
_____
_____
_____
_____
_____
_____
_____
_____
_____
_____
_____
_____
_____
_____
_____
_____
_____
_____
_____
_____
_____
_____
_____
_____
_____
_____
_____
_____
_____
_____
_____
_____

_____
_____

After Class, Write Test Review Note: Association Cues and Test Questions

1. After class, reread your class notes and condense them into Test Review Notes ✔

2. Choose a study area that is free of external and social distractions: _____ ✔

3. Eat a Power Study Snack to stay energized and focused (see list): _____ ✔

4. Manage your time.
   Estimate Time (Fantasy):   Start Time: Finish Time: Actual Time (Reality): ✔

5. Do the facts need further clarification (see textbook, tutoring center, or teacher)? ✔

6. To ace your test, use Association Cues to memorize the facts for Instant and Total Recall ✔

Fact: Create Association Cue for Instant and Total Recall

----

7. Visualize the test questions. Convert the facts into test questions ✔

Who? Where? When? What? Why?

My Class Notes

Date:

Topic:

Write down the Main Ideas and Supporting Details/Examples/Arguments:

_____

_____

_____

_____

_____

_____

_____

_____

_____

_____

_____

_____

_____

_____

_____

_____

_____

_____

_____

_____

_____

_____

_____

_____

_____

_____

_____

_____

_____

_____

_____

_____

_____

_____

After Class, Write Test Review Note: Association Cues and Test Questions

1. After class, reread your class notes and condense them into Test Review Notes ✓

2. Choose a study area that is free of external and social distractions: _____ ✓

3. Eat a Power Study Snack to stay energized and focused (see list): _____ ✓

4. Manage your time.
   Estimate Time (Fantasy):   Start Time: Finish Time: Actual Time (Reality): ✓

5. Do the facts need further clarification (see textbook, tutoring center, or teacher)? ✓

6. To ace your test, use Association Cues to memorize the facts for Instant and Total Recall ✓

Fact: Create Association Cue for Instant and Total Recall

- -

7. Visualize the test questions. Convert the facts into test questions ✓

Who? Where? When? What? Why?

My Class Notes

Date:

Topic:

Write down the Main Ideas and Supporting Details/Examples/Arguments:

After Class, Write Test Review Note: Association Cues and Test Questions

1. After class, reread your class notes and condense them into Test Review Notes ✔

2. Choose a study area that is free of external and social distractions: _____ ✔

3. Eat a Power Study Snack to stay energized and focused (see list): _____ ✔

4. Manage your time.
   Estimate Time (Fantasy):   Start Time: Finish Time: Actual Time (Reality): ✔

5. Do the facts need further clarification (see textbook, tutoring center, or teacher)? ✔

6. To ace your test, use Association Cues to memorize the facts for Instant and Total Recall ✔

Fact: Create Association Cue for Instant and Total Recall

- -

7. Visualize the test questions. Convert the facts into test questions ✔

Who? Where? When? What? Why?

My Class Notes

Date:

Topic:

Write down the Main Ideas and Supporting Details/Examples/Arguments:

_____

_____

_____

_____

_____

_____

_____

_____

_____

_____

_____

_____

_____

_____

_____

_____

_____

_____

_____

_____

_____

_____

_____

_____

_____

_____

_____

_____

_____

_____

_____

_____

_____

_____

After Class, Write Test Review Note: Association Cues and Test Questions

1. After class, reread your class notes and condense them into Test Review Notes ✓

2. Choose a study area that is free of external and social distractions: _____ ✓

3. Eat a Power Study Snack to stay energized and focused (see list): _____ ✓

4. Manage your time.
   Estimate Time (Fantasy):   Start Time: Finish Time: Actual Time (Reality): ✓

5. Do the facts need further clarification (see textbook, tutoring center, or teacher)? ✓

6. To ace your test, use Association Cues to memorize the facts for Instant and Total Recall ✓

Fact: Create Association Cue for Instant and Total Recall

----

7. Visualize the test questions. Convert the facts into test questions ✓

Who? Where? When? What? Why?

My Class Notes

Date:

Topic:

Write down the Main Ideas and Supporting Details/Examples/Arguments:

_____

_____

_____

_____

_____

_____

_____

_____

_____

_____

_____

_____

_____

_____

_____

_____

_____

_____

_____

_____

_____

_____

_____

_____

_____

_____

_____

_____

_____

_____

_____

_____

_____

After Class, Write Test Review Note: Association Cues and Test Questions

1. After class, reread your class notes and condense them into Test Review Notes ✔

2. Choose a study area that is free of external and social distractions: _____ ✔

3. Eat a Power Study Snack to stay energized and focused (see list): _____ ✔

4. Manage your time.
   Estimate Time (Fantasy):   Start Time: Finish Time: Actual Time (Reality): ✔

5. Do the facts need further clarification (see textbook, tutoring center, or teacher)? ✔

6. To ace your test, use Association Cues to memorize the facts for Instant and Total Recall ✔

Fact: Create Association Cue for Instant and Total Recall

- -

7. Visualize the test questions. Convert the facts into test questions ✔

Who? Where? When? What? Why?

My Class Notes

Date:

Topic:

Write down the Main Ideas and Supporting Details/Examples/Arguments:

_____

_____

_____

_____

_____

_____

_____

_____

_____

_____

_____

_____

_____

_____

_____

_____

_____

_____

_____

_____

_____

_____

_____

_____

_____

_____

_____

_____

_____

_____

_____

_____

_____

Write down the Main Ideas and Supporting Details/Examples/Arguments:

_____

After Class, Write Test Review Note: Association Cues and Test Questions

1. After class, reread your class notes and condense them into Test Review Notes ✔

2. Choose a study area that is free of external and social distractions: _____ ✔

3. Eat a Power Study Snack to stay energized and focused (see list): _____ ✔

4. Manage your time.
   Estimate Time (Fantasy):   Start Time: Finish Time: Actual Time (Reality): ✔

5. Do the facts need further clarification (see textbook, tutoring center, or teacher)? ✔

6. To ace your test, use Association Cues to memorize the facts for Instant and Total Recall ✔

Fact: Create Association Cue for Instant and Total Recall

----

7. Visualize the test questions. Convert the facts into test questions ✔

Who? Where? When? What? Why?

Date:

Topic:

Write down the Main Ideas and Supporting Details/Examples/Arguments:

Date:

Topic:

Write down the Main Ideas and Supporting Details/Examples/Arguments:

After Class, Write Test Review Note: Association Cues and Test Questions

1. After class, reread your class notes and condense them into Test Review Notes ✔

2. Choose a study area that is free of external and social distractions: _____ ✔

3. Eat a Power Study Snack to stay energized and focused (see list): _____ ✔

4. Manage your time.
    Estimate Time (Fantasy):   Start Time: Finish Time: Actual Time (Reality): ✔

5. Do the facts need further clarification (see textbook, tutoring center, or teacher)? ✔

6. To ace your test, use Association Cues to memorize the facts for Instant and Total Recall ✔

Fact: Create Association Cue for Instant and Total Recall

- -

7. Visualize the test questions. Convert the facts into test questions ✔

Who? Where? When? What? Why?

Date:

Topic:

Write down the Main Ideas and Supporting Details/Examples/Arguments:

_____

_____

_____

_____

_____

_____

_____

_____

_____

_____

_____

_____

_____

_____

_____

_____

_____

_____

_____

_____

_____

_____

_____

_____

_____

_____

_____

_____

_____

_____

Write down the Main Ideas and Supporting Details/Examples/Arguments:

After Class, Write Test Review Note: Association Cues and Test Questions

1. After class, reread your class notes and condense them into Test Review Notes ✔

2. Choose a study area that is free of external and social distractions: _____ ✔

3. Eat a Power Study Snack to stay energized and focused (see list): _____ ✔

4. Manage your time.
   Estimate Time (Fantasy):   Start Time: Finish Time: Actual Time (Reality): ✔

5. Do the facts need further clarification (see textbook, tutoring center, or teacher)? ✔

6. To ace your test, use Association Cues to memorize the facts for Instant and Total Recall ✔

Fact: Create Association Cue for Instant and Total Recall

----

7. Visualize the test questions. Convert the facts into test questions ✔

Who? Where? When? What? Why?

My Class Notes

Date:

Topic:

Write down the Main Ideas and Supporting Details/Examples/Arguments:

_____

_____

_____

_____

_____

_____

_____

_____

_____

_____

_____

_____

_____

_____

_____

_____

_____

_____

_____

_____

_____

_____

_____

_____

_____

_____

_____

_____

_____

_____

_____

_____

_____

_____

_____

_____

After Class, Write Test Review Note: Association Cues and Test Questions

1. After class, reread your class notes and condense them into Test Review Notes ✔

2. Choose a study area that is free of external and social distractions: _____ ✔

3. Eat a Power Study Snack to stay energized and focused (see list): _____ ✔

4. Manage your time.
   Estimate Time (Fantasy):   Start Time: Finish Time: Actual Time (Reality): ✔

5. Do the facts need further clarification (see textbook, tutoring center, or teacher)? ✔

6. To ace your test, use Association Cues to memorize the facts for Instant and Total Recall ✔

Fact: Create Association Cue for Instant and Total Recall

- -

7. Visualize the test questions. Convert the facts into test questions ✔

Who? Where? When? What? Why?

My Class Notes

Date:

Topic:

Write down the Main Ideas and Supporting Details/Examples/Arguments:

_____

_____

_____

_____

_____

_____

_____

_____

_____

_____

_____

_____

_____

_____

_____

_____

_____

_____

_____

_____

_____

_____

_____

_____

_____

_____

_____

_____

_____

_____

_____

After Class, Write Test Review Note: Association Cues and Test Questions

1. After class, reread your class notes and condense them into Test Review Notes ✓

2. Choose a study area that is free of external and social distractions: _____ ✓

3. Eat a Power Study Snack to stay energized and focused (see list): _____ ✓

4. Manage your time.
   Estimate Time (Fantasy):   Start Time: Finish Time: Actual Time (Reality): ✓

5. Do the facts need further clarification (see textbook, tutoring center, or teacher)? ✓

6. To ace your test, use Association Cues to memorize the facts for Instant and Total Recall ✓

Fact: Create Association Cue for Instant and Total Recall

----

7. Visualize the test questions. Convert the facts into test questions ✓

Who? Where? When? What? Why?

My Class Notes

Date:

Topic:

Write down the Main Ideas and Supporting Details/Examples/Arguments:

_____

_____

_____

_____

_____

_____

_____

_____

_____

_____

_____

_____

_____

_____

_____

_____

_____

_____

_____

_____

_____

_____

_____

_____

_____

_____

_____

_____

_____

_____

_____

_____

_____

After Class, Write Test Review Note: Association Cues and Test Questions

1. After class, reread your class notes and condense them into Test Review Notes ✔

2. Choose a study area that is free of external and social distractions: _____ ✔

3. Eat a Power Study Snack to stay energized and focused (see list): _____ ✔

4. Manage your time.
   Estimate Time (Fantasy):   Start Time: Finish Time: Actual Time (Reality): ✔

5. Do the facts need further clarification (see textbook, tutoring center, or teacher)? ✔

6. To ace your test, use Association Cues to memorize the facts for Instant and Total Recall ✔

Fact: Create Association Cue for Instant and Total Recall

----

7. Visualize the test questions. Convert the facts into test questions ✔

Who? Where? When? What? Why?

My Class Notes

Date:

Topic:

Write down the Main Ideas and Supporting Details/Examples/Arguments:

_____

_____

_____

_____

_____

_____

_____

_____

_____

_____

_____

_____

_____

_____

_____

_____

_____

_____

_____

_____

_____

_____

_____

_____

_____

_____

_____

_____

_____

_____

_____

_____

_____

_____

_____

_____

After Class, Write Test Review Note: Association Cues and Test Questions

1. After class, reread your class notes and condense them into Test Review Notes ✔

2. Choose a study area that is free of external and social distractions: _____ ✔

3. Eat a Power Study Snack to stay energized and focused (see list): _____ ✔

4. Manage your time.
   Estimate Time (Fantasy):   Start Time: Finish Time: Actual Time (Reality): ✔

5. Do the facts need further clarification (see textbook, tutoring center, or teacher)? ✔

6. To ace your test, use Association Cues to memorize the facts for Instant and Total Recall ✔

Fact: Create Association Cue for Instant and Total Recall

- -

7. Visualize the test questions. Convert the facts into test questions ✔

Who? Where? When? What? Why?

My Class Notes

Date:

Topic:

Write down the Main Ideas and Supporting Details/Examples/Arguments:

_____

_____

_____

_____

_____

_____

_____

_____

_____

_____

_____

_____

_____

_____

_____

_____

_____

_____

_____

_____

_____

_____

_____

_____

_____

_____

_____

_____

_____

_____

_____

_____

_____

After Class, Write Test Review Note: Association Cues and Test Questions

1. After class, reread your class notes and condense them into Test Review Notes ✔

2. Choose a study area that is free of external and social distractions: _____ ✔

3. Eat a Power Study Snack to stay energized and focused (see list): _____ ✔

4. Manage your time.
   Estimate Time (Fantasy):   Start Time: Finish Time: Actual Time (Reality): ✔

5. Do the facts need further clarification (see textbook, tutoring center, or teacher)? ✔

6. To ace your test, use Association Cues to memorize the facts for Instant and Total Recall ✔

Fact: Create Association Cue for Instant and Total Recall

- -

7. Visualize the test questions. Convert the facts into test questions ✔

Who? Where? When? What? Why?

My Class Notes

SMARTGRADES

Date:

Topic:

Write down the Main Ideas and Supporting Details/Examples/Arguments:

_____

_____

_____

_____

_____

_____

_____

_____

_____

_____

_____

_____

_____

_____

_____

_____

_____

_____

_____

_____

_____

_____

_____

_____

_____

_____

_____

_____

_____

_____

_____

_____

After Class, Write Test Review Note: Association Cues and Test Questions

1. After class, reread your class notes and condense them into Test Review Notes✔

2. Choose a study area that is free of external and social distractions: _____✔

3. Eat a Power Study Snack to stay energized and focused (see list): _____✔

4. Manage your time.
   Estimate Time (Fantasy):   Start Time: Finish Time: Actual Time (Reality):✔

5. Do the facts need further clarification (see textbook, tutoring center, or teacher)? ✔

6. To ace your test, use Association Cues to memorize the facts for Instant and Total Recall✔

Fact: Create Association Cue for Instant and Total Recall

- -

7. Visualize the test questions. Convert the facts into test questions ✔

Who? Where? When? What? Why?

My Class Notes

Date:

Topic:

Write down the Main Ideas and Supporting Details/Examples/Arguments:

After Class, Write Test Review Note: Association Cues and Test Questions

1. After class, reread your class notes and condense them into Test Review Notes ✔

2. Choose a study area that is free of external and social distractions: _____ ✔

3. Eat a Power Study Snack to stay energized and focused (see list): _____ ✔

4. Manage your time.
   Estimate Time (Fantasy):   Start Time: Finish Time: Actual Time (Reality): ✔

5. Do the facts need further clarification (see textbook, tutoring center, or teacher)? ✔

6. To ace your test, use Association Cues to memorize the facts for Instant and Total Recall ✔

Fact: Create Association Cue for Instant and Total Recall

----

7. Visualize the test questions. Convert the facts into test questions ✔

Who? Where? When? What? Why?

My Class Notes

Date:

Topic:

Write down the Main Ideas and Supporting Details/Examples/Arguments:

_____

_____

_____

_____

_____

_____

_____

_____

_____

_____

_____

_____

_____

_____

_____

_____

_____

_____

_____

_____

_____

_____

_____

_____

_____

_____

_____

_____

_____

_____

_____

_____

_____

_____

_____

_____

_____

After Class, Write Test Review Note: Association Cues and Test Questions

1. After class, reread your class notes and condense them into Test Review Notes ✓

2. Choose a study area that is free of external and social distractions: _____ ✓

3. Eat a Power Study Snack to stay energized and focused (see list): _____ ✓

4. Manage your time.
   Estimate Time (Fantasy):   Start Time: Finish Time: Actual Time (Reality): ✓

5. Do the facts need further clarification (see textbook, tutoring center, or teacher)? ✓

6. To ace your test, use Association Cues to memorize the facts for Instant and Total Recall ✓

Fact: Create Association Cue for Instant and Total Recall

----

7. Visualize the test questions. Convert the facts into test questions ✓

Who? Where? When? What? Why?

My Class Notes

Date:

Topic:

Write down the Main Ideas and Supporting Details/Examples/Arguments:

After Class, Write Test Review Note: Association Cues and Test Questions

1. After class, reread your class notes and condense them into Test Review Notes ✔

2. Choose a study area that is free of external and social distractions: _____ ✔

3. Eat a Power Study Snack to stay energized and focused (see list): _____ ✔

4. Manage your time.
   Estimate Time (Fantasy):   Start Time: Finish Time: Actual Time (Reality): ✔

5. Do the facts need further clarification (see textbook, tutoring center, or teacher)? ✔

6. To ace your test, use Association Cues to memorize the facts for Instant and Total Recall ✔

Fact: Create Association Cue for Instant and Total Recall

----

7. Visualize the test questions. Convert the facts into test questions ✔

Who? Where? When? What? Why?

My Class Notes

Date:

Topic:

Write down the Main Ideas and Supporting Details/Examples/Arguments:

_____
_____
_____
_____
_____
_____
_____
_____
_____
_____
_____
_____
_____
_____
_____
_____
_____
_____
_____
_____
_____
_____
_____
_____
_____
_____
_____
_____
_____
_____
_____
_____
_____
_____

After Class, Write Test Review Note: Association Cues and Test Questions

1. After class, reread your class notes and condense them into Test Review Notes ✔

2. Choose a study area that is free of external and social distractions: _____ ✔

3. Eat a Power Study Snack to stay energized and focused (see list): _____ ✔

4. Manage your time.
   Estimate Time (Fantasy):   Start Time: Finish Time: Actual Time (Reality): ✔

5. Do the facts need further clarification (see textbook, tutoring center, or teacher)? ✔

6. To ace your test, use Association Cues to memorize the facts for Instant and Total Recall ✔

Fact: Create Association Cue for Instant and Total Recall

----

7. Visualize the test questions. Convert the facts into test questions ✔

Who? Where? When? What? Why?

My Class Notes

Date:

Topic:

Write down the Main Ideas and Supporting Details/Examples/Arguments:

_____

_____

_____

_____

_____

_____

_____

_____

_____

_____

_____

_____

_____

_____

_____

_____

_____

_____

_____

_____

_____

_____

_____

_____

_____

_____

_____

_____

_____

_____

_____

_____

_____

_____

After Class, Write Test Review Note: Association Cues and Test Questions

1. After class, reread your class notes and condense them into Test Review Notes ✔

2. Choose a study area that is free of external and social distractions: _____ ✔

3. Eat a Power Study Snack to stay energized and focused (see list): _____ ✔

4. Manage your time.
    Estimate Time (Fantasy):   Start Time: Finish Time: Actual Time (Reality): ✔

5. Do the facts need further clarification (see textbook, tutoring center, or teacher)? ✔

6. To ace your test, use Association Cues to memorize the facts for Instant and Total Recall ✔

Fact: Create Association Cue for Instant and Total Recall

----

7. Visualize the test questions. Convert the facts into test questions ✔

Who? Where? When? What? Why?

My Class Notes   **SMARTGRADES**

Date:

Topic:

Write down the Main Ideas and Supporting Details/Examples/Arguments:

_____

_____

_____

_____

_____

_____

_____

_____

_____

_____

_____

_____

_____

_____

_____

_____

_____

_____

_____

_____

_____

_____

_____

_____

_____

_____

_____

_____

_____

_____

_____

_____

_____

_____

_____

After Class, Write Test Review Note: Association Cues and Test Questions

1. After class, reread your class notes and condense them into Test Review Notes ✔

2. Choose a study area that is free of external and social distractions: _____ ✔

3. Eat a Power Study Snack to stay energized and focused (see list): _____ ✔

4. Manage your time.
   Estimate Time (Fantasy):   Start Time: Finish Time: Actual Time (Reality): ✔

5. Do the facts need further clarification (see textbook, tutoring center, or teacher)? ✔

6. To ace your test, use Association Cues to memorize the facts for Instant and Total Recall ✔

Fact: Create Association Cue for Instant and Total Recall

- -

7. Visualize the test questions. Convert the facts into test questions ✔

Who? Where? When? What? Why?

My Class Notes

Date:

Topic:

Write down the Main Ideas and Supporting Details/Examples/Arguments:

_____

_____

_____

_____

_____

_____

_____

_____

_____

_____

_____

_____

_____

_____

_____

_____

_____

_____

_____

_____

_____

_____

_____

_____

_____

_____

_____

_____

_____

_____

_____

_____

_____

_____

After Class, Write Test Review Note: Association Cues and Test Questions

1. After class, reread your class notes and condense them into Test Review Notes ✔

2. Choose a study area that is free of external and social distractions: _____ ✔

3. Eat a Power Study Snack to stay energized and focused (see list): _____ ✔

4. Manage your time.
   Estimate Time (Fantasy):   Start Time: Finish Time: Actual Time (Reality): ✔

5. Do the facts need further clarification (see textbook, tutoring center, or teacher)? ✔

6. To ace your test, use Association Cues to memorize the facts for Instant and Total Recall ✔

Fact: Create Association Cue for Instant and Total Recall

- -

7. Visualize the test questions. Convert the facts into test questions ✔

Who? Where? When? What? Why?

My Class Notes

Date:

Topic:

Write down the Main Ideas and Supporting Details/Examples/Arguments:

_____

_____

_____

_____

_____

_____

_____

_____

_____

_____

_____

_____

_____

_____

_____

_____

_____

_____

_____

_____

_____

_____

_____

_____

_____

_____

_____

_____

_____

_____

_____

_____

_____

After Class, Write Test Review Note: Association Cues and Test Questions

1. After class, reread your class notes and condense them into Test Review Notes ✓

2. Choose a study area that is free of external and social distractions: _____ ✓

3. Eat a Power Study Snack to stay energized and focused (see list): _____ ✓

4. Manage your time.
   Estimate Time (Fantasy):   Start Time: Finish Time: Actual Time (Reality): ✓

5. Do the facts need further clarification (see textbook, tutoring center, or teacher)? ✓

6. To ace your test, use Association Cues to memorize the facts for Instant and Total Recall ✓

Fact: Create Association Cue for Instant and Total Recall

----

7. Visualize the test questions. Convert the facts into test questions ✓

Who? Where? When? What? Why?

My Class Notes

Date:

Topic:

Write down the Main Ideas and Supporting Details/Examples/Arguments:

After Class, Write Test Review Note: Association Cues and Test Questions

1. After class, reread your class notes and condense them into Test Review Notes ✔

2. Choose a study area that is free of external and social distractions: _____ ✔

3. Eat a Power Study Snack to stay energized and focused (see list): _____ ✔

4. Manage your time.
   Estimate Time (Fantasy):   Start Time: Finish Time: Actual Time (Reality): ✔

5. Do the facts need further clarification (see textbook, tutoring center, or teacher)? ✔

6. To ace your test, use Association Cues to memorize the facts for Instant and Total Recall ✔

Fact: Create Association Cue for Instant and Total Recall

- -

7. Visualize the test questions. Convert the facts into test questions ✔

Who? Where? When? What? Why?

My Class Notes

Date:

Topic:

Write down the Main Ideas and Supporting Details/Examples/Arguments:

After Class, Write Test Review Note: Association Cues and Test Questions

1. After class, reread your class notes and condense them into Test Review Notes ✓

2. Choose a study area that is free of external and social distractions: _____ ✓

3. Eat a Power Study Snack to stay energized and focused (see list): _____ ✓

4. Manage your time.
   Estimate Time (Fantasy):   Start Time: Finish Time: Actual Time (Reality): ✓

5. Do the facts need further clarification (see textbook, tutoring center, or teacher)? ✓

6. To ace your test, use Association Cues to memorize the facts for Instant and Total Recall ✓

Fact: Create Association Cue for Instant and Total Recall

----

7. Visualize the test questions. Convert the facts into test questions ✓

Who? Where? When? What? Why?

My Class Notes

Date:

Topic:

Write down the Main Ideas and Supporting Details/Examples/Arguments:

_____

_____

_____

_____

_____

_____

_____

_____

_____

_____

_____

_____

_____

_____

_____

_____

_____

_____

_____

_____

_____

_____

_____

_____

_____

_____

_____

_____

_____

_____

_____

_____

_____

_____

My Class Notes

Date:

Write down the Main Ideas and Supporting Details/Examples/Arguments:

_____

_____

After Class, Write Test Review Note: Association Cues and Test Questions

1. After class, reread your class notes and condense them into Test Review Notes ✔

2. Choose a study area that is free of external and social distractions: _____ ✔

3. Eat a Power Study Snack to stay energized and focused (see list): _____ ✔

4. Manage your time.
   Estimate Time (Fantasy):   Start Time: Finish Time: Actual Time (Reality): ✔

5. Do the facts need further clarification (see textbook, tutoring center, or teacher)? ✔

6. To ace your test, use Association Cues to memorize the facts for Instant and Total Recall ✔

Fact: Create Association Cue for Instant and Total Recall

----

7. Visualize the test questions. Convert the facts into test questions ✔

Who? Where? When? What? Why?

My Class Notes

Date:

Topic:

Write down the Main Ideas and Supporting Details/Examples/Arguments:

After Class, Write Test Review Note: Association Cues and Test Questions

1. After class, reread your class notes and condense them into Test Review Notes ✔

2. Choose a study area that is free of external and social distractions: _____ ✔

3. Eat a Power Study Snack to stay energized and focused (see list): _____ ✔

4. Manage your time.
   Estimate Time (Fantasy):   Start Time: Finish Time: Actual Time (Reality): ✔

5. Do the facts need further clarification (see textbook, tutoring center, or teacher)? ✔

6. To ace your test, use Association Cues to memorize the facts for Instant and Total Recall ✔

Fact: Create Association Cue for Instant and Total Recall

----

7. Visualize the test questions. Convert the facts into test questions ✔

Who? Where? When? What? Why?

Date:

Topic:

Write down the Main Ideas and Supporting Details/Examples/Arguments:

_____

_____

_____

_____

_____

_____

_____

_____

_____

_____

_____

_____

_____

_____

_____

_____

_____

_____

_____

_____

_____

_____

_____

_____

_____

_____

_____

_____

_____

_____

_____

_____

_____

_____

After Class, Write Test Review Note: Association Cues and Test Questions

1. After class, reread your class notes and condense them into Test Review Notes ✔

2. Choose a study area that is free of external and social distractions: _____ ✔

3. Eat a Power Study Snack to stay energized and focused (see list): _____ ✔

4. Manage your time.
   Estimate Time (Fantasy):   Start Time: Finish Time: Actual Time (Reality): ✔

5. Do the facts need further clarification (see textbook, tutoring center, or teacher)? ✔

6. To ace your test, use Association Cues to memorize the facts for Instant and Total Recall ✔

Fact: Create Association Cue for Instant and Total Recall

----

7. Visualize the test questions. Convert the facts into test questions ✔

Who? Where? When? What? Why?

Our Power Study Snack Suggestions

Choose One of Our Power Study Snacks or Create Your Own Energy Menu

1. Nutritious Pizza
    Whole Wheat Pita, Mozzarella Cheese Slice, Tomato Slice, Basil Leaf, and
    Olive Oil, Microwave 30 Seconds

2. Humus and Veggies
    Carrots, Celery, Broccoli, Red Peppers . . .

3. Bran Muffin
    Apple-Oat, Cranberry-Walnut, Banana-Pecan . . .

4. Sports Bar with 10+ Grams of Protein
    Avoid High Amounts of Saturated Fat or Hydrogenated Vegetable Oils

5. A Small 3oz. Can of Tuna/Sardines with 4-6 Whole Grain Crackers

6. One Container of Low Fat Yogurt Sprinkled with High Fiber Cereal and
    Fresh Fruit

7. Whole-Grain Cereal with Fat Free or 1% Low Fat Milk and Fresh Fruit

8. Trail Mix: Your Favorite Nuts
    Peanuts, Almonds, Cashews, Pistachios with Raisins and Cranberries . . .

9. Dried Fruit Mix: Your Favorite Fruits
    Apricots, Pineapple, Apple Chips, Banana Chips . . .

10. Vegetable Soup and a Slice of Whole Grain Bread

11. Chocolate Smoothie: Chocolate Soy Milk, Peanut Butter, and Whey
    Protein

12. Oatmeal-Raisin Cookie

My Power Study Snacks

List Your Favorite Power Study Snacks to Stay Energized and Focused

1. _____

2. _____

3. _____

4. _____

5. _____

6. _____

7. _____

8. _____

9. _____

10. _____

PHOTON
SUPERHERO of EDUCATION ®

EVERY
DAY
AN
EASY A

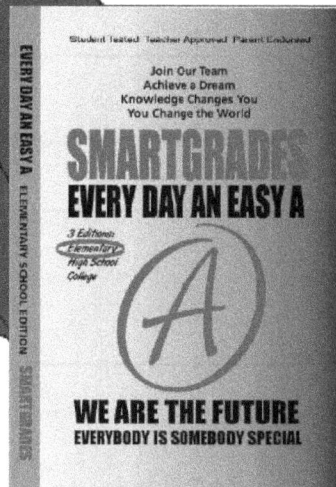

EVERY DAY AN EASY A
3 Editions: Elementary, High School, College
ACE EVERY TEST EVERY TIME
All Global Bookstores

www.BooksNotBombs.com
EVERYBODY IS SOMEBODY SPECIAL

---

1 Minute Time Management Class
10 Steps to Success
EVERY DAY AN EASY A ©All Rights Reserved, 2010.

Step 1 ❏
Make a Daily Action Plan
Write Down Your Big Goals

Step 2 ❏
Set Your Priorities
Urgent, Important, Low, and Optional

Step 3 ❏
Breakdown Your Dreams
Breakdown Big Goal into Smaller Steps
List Steps Necessary to Complete Big Goal

Step 4 ❏
Divide and Conquer
Take Baby Steps Toward Reaching Goal
Crawl. Walk. Fly. Soar...

Step 5 ❏
Use Time Logs: Estimated Vs. Actual Time
e.g., Estimate Time for Lunch: 1 Hour
Actual Time: 20 Minutes
40 Minutes for Errands: Bank, Post Office, Store

Step 6 ❏
Life Is a Bumpy Road
Make Time for Delays, Detours,
Distractions, and Disappointments
e.g., Copier Runs Out of Toner and Paper

Step 7 ❏
Use Checkboxes to Keep Track of Completed Tasks

Step 8 ❏
Review and Refine Daily Action Plan
Pay Attention to Strengths and Weaknesses

Step 9 ❏
Celebrate Your Success
Celebrate Job Well Done with Daily Reward

Step 10 ❏
EVERY DAY AN EASY A
www.everydayaneasya.com

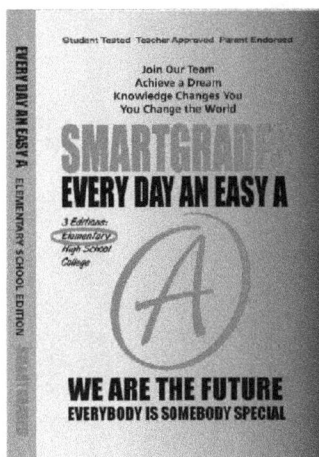

www.ingramcontent.com/pod-product-compliance
Lightning Source LLC
Chambersburg PA
CBHW081331090426
42737CB00017B/3098